STARTING SCHOOL RIGHT

How do I plan for a successful first week in my classroom?

Otis
KRIEGEL

 Alexandria, VA USA

Website: www.ascd.org
E-mail: books@ascd.org

www.ascdarias.org

Printed in the United States of America. ASCD publications present a variety of viewpoints. The views expressed or implied in this book should not be interpreted as official positions of the Association.

ASCD®, ASCD LEARN TEACH LEAD®, ASCD ARIAS™, and ANSWERS YOU NEED FROM VOICES YOU TRUST® are trademarks owned by ASCD and may not be used without permission. All other referenced trademarks are the property of their respective owners.

PAPERBACK ISBN: 978-1-4166-2140-9   ASCD product #SF116009

Also available as an e-book (see Books in Print for the ISBNs).

Library of Congress Cataloging-in-Publication Data

Names: Kriegel, Otis, author.
Title: Starting school right : how do I plan for a successful first week in my classroom? / Otis Kriegel.
Description: Alexandria, Virginia : ASCD, [2016]
Identifiers: LCCN 2015045566 (print) | LCCN 2016001547 (ebook) | ISBN 9781416621409 (pbk.) | ISBN 9781416621416 (Kindle/MOBI) | ISBN 9781416621423 (PDF) | ISBN 9781416621430 (EPUB)
Subjects: LCSH: First year teachers--United States. | Classroom management--United States.
Classification: LCC LB2844.1.N4 K75 2016 (print) | LCC LB2844.1.N4 (ebook) |
    DDC 371.1--dc23
LC record available at http://lccn.loc.gov/2015045566

24 23 22 21 20 19 18 17 16   1 2 3 4 5 6 7 8 9 10

STARTING SCHOOL RIGHT

How do I plan for a successful first week in my classroom?

Want to earn a free ASCD Arias e-book?
Your opinion counts! Please take 2–3 minutes to give
us your feedback on this publication. All survey
respondents will be entered into a drawing to
win an ASCD Arias e-book.

Please visit
www.ascd.org/ariasfeedback

Thank you!

The First Week Really Does Matter

As I was celebrating the end of graduate school and completing student teaching, every veteran teacher, principal, and professor encouraged me to start getting ready for my first week of teaching school next fall. These educators warned me that my survival, success, and stamina all depended on the first week of school. They cautioned that everything—parent–teacher conferences, a field trip in November, an experiment in March, and even testing—depended on a successful first week of school.

Like most student teachers, I began my practicum after that school year had started so I didn't have any firsthand experience with how to get the ball rolling. What did these professionals know that I didn't about the first week of school? And what should I do in May to prepare for September?

Is the first week of school that crucial? You bet it is.

Does the success of your entire school year depend upon it? No. But there are systems to put in place and strategies to use that can help you prepare a positive structure for the year. The systems and strategies that you implement during the first week of school—and continue to review and reinforce daily over the next month—will allow your students to feel comfortable with your expectations and will assist you in becoming a better educator.

In this book you'll find many strategies to help both you and your students start the year right. Most important, you will be guided in planning the beginning of the school year and thinking about how you define and achieve success in your classroom.

Every teacher in the country starts the year off a bit differently. Even if the scripts were the same, each teacher would express it differently according to his or her personality, in part by emphasizing different words and speaking at a different volume. Teaching *is* personal. Consider as many ideas as you can, but make sure that the ideas and systems you plan to use feel genuine. Otherwise, you'll implement a bunch of systems and ideas that you won't be able to stick with because they won't be authentic. Starting school right depends on knowing your competencies and weaknesses, along with your preferences and aversions.

The first week is meant to be exciting and fun, though you'll make more than a few mistakes. Don't let that get in the way of the thrill of starting the 10-month school-year journey.

This book does not provide a script to follow. Rather, it offers ideas so that you can figure out what works for you and what makes the first week of school the foundation of a terrific year. Read it straight through or find sections that are relevant to the issue you are dealing with today. Good luck—and enjoy the journey.

Survey Your Classroom

The week before school starts can be nerve-racking. Your mind races among multiple to-do lists, from figuring out how to set up the classroom to learning your students' names. The pressure may be daunting even to experienced teachers. It may surprise you that being a veteran teacher doesn't make the first week any easier. In fact, the pressure of having finished the last school year with an incredible class can make the expectations for the upcoming year overwhelming.

Now that you've been assigned a classroom, how can you make that room of random furniture and odds and ends feel like a place you want to live in? Here is what we will cover:

- Merging the classroom and your style
- Creating pathways
- Considering students' experiences

Merging the Classroom and Your Style

You cannot plan the set up for your classroom without seeing the room. What does the room offer? Make a drawing and note things that cannot be moved, including windows, doors, closets, built-in shelves or cubbies, whiteboards, pencil sharpeners, and sinks. Sometimes there are some absurdly useless pieces of furniture built into classrooms, such as oversized desks, shelves that are not as deep as a crayon, or whiteboards that face only a third of the classroom. Also, note if the afternoon glare from the sun makes it difficult to work in certain areas. Can you install a window covering? Is it a warm room? Do the windows open or can you use a fan? Is the room near the recess yard and noisy? Is it near the bathrooms?

Next, find out what furniture is being offered and investigate whether you have tables, desks, or maybe even beanbags to work into the mix. Once you know what is available, ask yourself questions that merge the design of the room with how you teach or envision yourself teaching in this space. Is your room ideally arranged for your preferences, including the following:

- Supporting a collaborative learning environment or individual learning?
- Teaching in small or large groups?
- Teaching in a student-centered or teacher-driven environment?
- Assigning a specific work space to each student or allowing each student to work where he or she wants?

If your room has individual desks, cluster them in small or large groups or place them independently. If you favor a mix of individual and collaborative learning, arrange the desks as you want students to start the first morning, yet consider how the furniture can be moved to form and disband groups.

Depending on the shape and size of the desks as they relate to the room, you can cluster them in groups of two to five. Clusters are terrific for small groups—they're like little satellites around the classroom. If you want fewer (and larger) groups, arrange the desks so that the writing surfaces are in longer rows facing each other.

It is a rare classroom that has tables, but stranger things have happened. One year I was assigned large desks with tiny chairs. When my upper elementary students sat down, their chins were at the level of the desks. They brought in pillows to use as boosters until we switched with an early elementary class that had bigger chairs. The early elementary students were using the big chairs as jungle gyms because their feet didn't touch the floor when they sat in them.

Tables are great for collaborative learning. Your students can sit in groups around each table. If you want more individual space for students to work, position chairs on only one side of a table.

Cathalya, a veteran middle school teacher, doesn't let herself get boxed into one type of classroom. She tells me, "Luckily these desks aren't bolted to the floor. Then I'd be in real trouble. The students sit at individual desks so they can work independently if needed. But when I want them to work in groups, they scoot a few feet to the left or right, or sometimes they turn around and join others. I have the best of both worlds!"

Creating Pathways

Organize your room to reflect who you are as a teacher—a sitter or a sprinter. Do you anticipate sitting at a desk or computer or moving around the classroom as you teach? And keep referring to those simple questions about how you want students to learn (in the previous section). Do you want students to collaborate in small or large groups? Work independently? Do you anticipate the learning to be teacher driven or student centered? Are the work spaces assigned? How you arrange the furniture will allow students to quickly grasp the type of learning environment in which you expect them to thrive.

Addressing the concept of a student-centered classroom versus a teacher-driven classroom depends on how much talking to the class as a whole group you want to do. Do you want everyone facing the front of the room where you teach? Or will you teach from multiple places in the room, such as at clusters of desks or tables? If you prefer a lecture-style classroom, arrange the desks to face you at whatever spot you think you'll be teaching from the most. If you think you will teach in multiple areas, then desk orientation won't matter as much. Your students can turn to face you when needed.

Whether your classroom is stocked with tables or desks, you can start the year with assigned seats and (if you choose) work toward allowing the students to find a location that works best for them. Or, you can assign seats and rotate them throughout the year. The school year is long so you don't need to make that decision right now, but you do need to decide how to begin. If you let students choose their own seats it may be a bit chaotic, but you will discover who is friends with whom, who wants to hide in the back of the classroom, and which kids need to be encouraged to join the classroom community. If you and your students are all new to the school (such as with a new school or the earliest grade level in the school), using labels to assign seats offers students reassurance that they are in the right place and may help them begin to develop a sense of belonging. The first moments in a new classroom can be scary and potentially emotionally scarring for some students. Also, if you are the new one to the community, prepare to be schooled by some students who will try to take advantage of you by sitting with their friends and chatting all day.

As you arrange the furniture, ensure that you are creating pathways so that students can get materials from their backpacks and to sharpen a pencil with ease. Otherwise, traffic jams will create frustration for both you and your students—and those tight spaces will instigate avoidable social confrontations and mayhem. You may be shocked at how quickly a bump or shove on the way to or from the pencil sharpener can alter a perfectly peaceful afternoon.

As you work out the details of your space, remember that students may be bringing in classroom supplies (paper towels, glue, or tissues) during the first few weeks of school. You may want to provide a few crates where they can easily drop off these materials—again, without creating a traffic jam.

After 12 years of teaching 1st through 5th grades, I took a position at a middle school to create a digital arts program. I was excited about the challenge, the change of environment, and the age group. Over the summer, I created the curriculum with a mix of different projects. I planned to teach one project at a time. Later, however, I discovered that the space I was assigned was not a traditional classroom. It was the library broken up into four distinct areas: the stacks (bookshelves), six large tables that could hold about 30 students, a large open area where the entire class could meet, and a computer lab with eight desktop computers. Once I saw the layout, I immediately changed my plan. If I didn't, I would have been squeezing all 35 students at tables where they would have been practically sitting on top of one another without enough room for their laptops or elbows.

Instead, I relied on my experience as an elementary school teacher. I used the open area for a general meeting to start class and the tables to teach the whole class. I separated the class into three learning groups that would rotate through the open area, the tables, and the computer lab. I made the stacks off-limits because I wanted to be able to see all students at all times. In each area, a small group would work on a project. I floated among the areas, supporting individual or small group work and teaching mini lessons. The space transformed the entire curriculum and the way I taught.

Instead of fighting the space that you are assigned, make the most of it and dance with it. Sometimes the space you are assigned can be an inspiration on how to teach a class. Be open to it.

Considering Students' Experiences

Depending upon the grade and the school, students will arrive with different expectations and various needs. Here are key questions to answer about your students that will affect the way you prepare your classroom:

- Are your students new to the school? Is this their first experience at school?
- Are your students graduating this year from the school? Do they have "top dog" attitudes or have they "checked out"?

Answering these questions will help you to think about how your students may react to your classroom design and what you can do to prepare for their responses.

If you are teaching a grade that will serve as most students' first experience in the school, or if you are new to a school and your style is different than what the students are accustomed to, you'll need to be very clear about expectations. For example, when I taught 1st grade, I knew the students were coming from a structured kindergarten classroom and the organization of my classroom would not be a surprise to my students. But when I taught digital arts in middle school, I aimed to provide the students with far more freedom and independence than they were used to. I started out with a very structured classroom and eased them into being more self-directed.

Looping with students. Even if students are looping with you, it's important to assume that they will remember little of the classroom systems that you developed together the year before. Summer vacation is long and can do strange things to memory, whether you're a teacher or a student.

At one school, I taught a multiage class of 4th and 5th graders. At the end of their 5th grade year, those students would go to a new 6th grade teacher. The newly promoted 5th graders would stay with me for their second year and we'd integrate a new cohort of 4th graders into our classroom. How did this affect the way I taught and set up my classroom? The difference was enormous! The returning students acted as ambassadors to the classroom systems and set up everything for the incoming students. I barely unpacked my room—the students did it for me. When I returned to a more traditional classroom assignment of all new students each year, I started the school year with minimal classroom systems so that I could slowly teach the students how the classroom worked. By week two or three, everyone was on the same page. Well, not quite. But almost!

Checklist

What should you consider when planning your classroom layout for the start of school?

- ☐ Merging the classroom and your style
- ☐ Creating pathways
- ☐ Considering students' experiences

Now that your classroom is set up, let's talk about implementing a management style the first week of school.

Understand Yourself as a Teacher

You put your soul into teaching every day, as do your colleagues. Many teachers choose the profession because it is a powerful way to give back the community; others because they believe it is the best way to fight for social justice; some because they simply love the craft and the practice of being a teacher. I have also met teachers who were directly inspired by their own teachers—and others who chose the profession because they wanted to provide a better education than they received to their students. Whatever the reason for being a teacher, your personality, sense of humor or lack thereof, the cadence with which you speak, your physical presence, and the sound of your voice will affect the way you teach and the way students respond to you. Teaching is a lot like acting. On stage or in the classroom, you must keep your personal life separate from the role you play, but who you are comes through and characterizes every performance.

Learn to be comfortable with your role before the first week of school starts. It's as important to identify the type of teacher you are, or aspire to be, as it is to know what you are teaching. In this section we will cover the following topics:

- Using your personality as a tool
- Speaking in your natural voice
- Ensuring students' well-being
- Adjusting and adapting—everything

Using Your Personality as a Tool

Ask yourself the following questions before the first week of school so that your teaching style reflects your strengths. Your answers will help you create a plan for the first week that feels genuine and your students will learn about you by the consistency of your actions.

- **Speaking:** Are you loud and boisterous? Never stop talking? Can you speak louder than a subway car as it passes by? Or, are you quiet and soft spoken? Does it need to be quiet enough to hear a pin drop in the classroom for students to hear your voice?
- **Joking or not:** Do you use humor and make jokes or are you more of a straight talker?
- **Loving or hating technology:** Are you fond of technology and use a pile of devices to connect with your students or are you fearful of technology and find even a whiteboard intimidating?
- **Considering the environment:** Do you work best when everything is neat, organized, and orderly or do you thrive in controlled chaos?

Speaking in Your Natural Voice

A former colleague, Ted, always said that the most important lesson on the first day of school was for his students to learn to recognize his voice and tone. He would speak to them as he would for the rest of the year, modeling how he expected them to communicate with each other. A naturally quiet-natured man, he would raise his voice some, but the first week was a

*chance, as he said, "to teach the kids what they would hear
from me in terms of tone and cadence of speech. I wanted
to provide them a window into what they could expect for
the rest of the year." Ted also said that by starting this way, if
he ever did get frustrated and raise his voice, it was treated
as out of the ordinary and worked well to restore order very
quickly.*

Don't fake it and use what you think should be a "teacher's voice." That's absurd and won't work for long. Using
your natural voice may sound obvious, but it is essential
to training your new students to understand who you are
and to get used to both your voice and temperament. It lets
them know what to expect—and leads into how you plan to
manage your class.

Ensuring Students' Well-being

In every class I try to form a student-centered classroom.
My goal is to empower students, which I believe helps them
take control of their own learning. I think it is important that
students know I will always listen to them and consider their
ideas. But, at the end of the day, if something arises that has
to do with safety, whether physical or emotional, or if there
is a change required because of the curriculum, the class
becomes a democratic dictatorship. We all get a vote and
must respect one another but when it comes down to certain
decisions, the teacher must make the call. It isn't out of lack
of respect for the agreed-upon system. Instead it is about the
teacher's responsibility to students and to their families. Our

role as teachers is to be prepared to make tough decisions, many of them on the fly. Trust yourself to make good, on-the-spot calls, but then be sure to reflect upon them later so you are more prepared for similar situations in the future.

Adjusting and Adapting—Everything

What happens the first week doesn't need to be etched in stone. Restaurants adapt recipes to make them better. Cities are built, destroyed, and rebuilt. Laws are created, rewritten, and revised. So use the first week to form the rules or guidelines of the classroom society and follow them. In a few weeks or a few months, you can change them if you and your students have outgrown them. Make the rules work for the classroom, which means being honest if they need to be changed or removed. Stay aware as the year progresses. What works in September may not work in May.

I use the first week to establish classroom guidelines and a month later, or sometimes sooner, I revisit those guidelines with the whole class or in small groups to evaluate whether they are working. Sometimes we leave them alone, other times we rewrite the entire constitution. It is so exciting! Students say, "It seems absurd now that we must line up with the same partner for a week. Maybe when we first formed the rule it made sense, but we don't need that reminder anymore. We know each other now!" If we reach consensus, we delete the rule. Other times students might say, "I think we need to add a guideline about [whatever they felt was not going well]." And of course, if I want an addition or a deletion, I chime in. Reviewing the guidelines makes the classroom a living, breathing organism that changes as we evolve.

Checklist

- ☐ Using your personality as a tool
- ☐ Speaking in your natural voice
- ☐ Ensuring students' well-being
- ☐ Adjusting and adapting—everything

"OK," you say, "but how do I begin to move forward to implement any of this in my classroom? What do I say first?" Let's keep that simple—and you'll find that advice in the next section.

Establish the Basics

Your students have arrived! You've helped your new students find their assigned seats or choose their own. Backpacks are put away, whether hanging on the backs of their chairs or in the hallway (may depend upon the school's rules). Classroom supplies have been placed into crates and are out of the way.

Everyone is silent. Twenty-five (or more) pairs of eyes are staring at you. This is the quietest your class might be all year. You stare back, knowing and feeling that everyone is apprehensive but hoping for the best. Now what?

You think about the tidbits of information that you want and need to get across to them. You wish you could do it without talking, but watching your students isn't going to get the job done. Think about when you board an airplane. What's among the first pieces of information the flight attendants share with you? They provide information about how to exit the aircraft, use the seat belts, respond to an emergency, find the bathrooms (and when you can use them), and call for help. Without that basic information, passengers would have a lot of questions—and many still act as if they don't know the rules.

Assume nothing. Explain the basics. Let's take a hard look at the things you'll need to explain right away so that everyone is on the same page.

- Signaling
- Wrangling, not strangling
- Establishing routines
- Taking a load off

"When I am mentoring new teachers, and I mean brand new, I always ask what they want to achieve on the first day and the first week of school. They always give me an answer that they think I want to hear," laughs Wesley, a veteran teacher and K–8 principal. "After they list all the academic and curricular activities they expect to cover, I ask them how the kids will know how to do any of these things, even if a teacher loops [teaches a group of students for two consecutive grades] with a class. Assuming children will somehow already know the classroom routines is asking for trouble. You have to cover

the basics first, and I mean basics! How many people exit the bus out the wrong door? We all need reminders. Kids need reminders in the beginning of the school year. I tell teachers, both vets and rookies, to lay off the curriculum and develop a smooth-running classroom the first week of school so everyone knows where to get a pencil, how to treat one another, and what to do if they need to go to the bathroom. A teacher who covers the basics always impresses me."

The first item of business is to establish how you can get students' attention and how they can get yours. Whether you use a call and response, a bell, or a clap, make sure they know the signal. And if you want them to raise their hands, feet, or both hands and feet to get your attention and ask a question, you must establish that as well.

Signaling for Attention

The absolute first aspect of management I establish is how I will get everyone's attention. I'm loud and have a big voice, so I use a call and response where I say something, a chant of some sort ("chocolate chips"), and students respond ("and milk"). Some teachers use a bell or a rain stick—something that can be used to capture attention that doesn't rely on their voice. Some teachers employ clapping, stomping, or other body language cues, such as beginning to quietly tap their shoulders. Other teachers prefer that students mime applause. Slowly, everyone in the class sees the signal and begins to respond. Whatever you choose will catch on quickly and serve as an effective, easy way to gain the attention of your students.

After you have determined how you want to get your students' attention, you'll need to set up a way for them to get yours. To avoid having all students attempt to talk to you at once (over each other), choose a method for your students to get your attention, whether it is raising a hand, placing a pinky on the nose, holding a thumb in the air, or using another signal that you invent. Put it into practice the first day and establish its power and meaning the first week.

Establishing consistent routines for engaging everyone's attention and giving your attention to a student are two of the most crucial aspects of management to achieve during the first week of school, if not the first day. Practice it throughout the first day and the first week to ensure everyone understands and remembers it.

Establishing guidelines. You better know where those bathrooms are. Now. And you need to learn if there are any general school rules about their use, such as signing out hall passes. I guarantee that there will be a kid bouncing, wincing, and waving her hands within 10 minutes. A few kids will know that at the start of the year they might be able to sneak out to the bathroom and stay there to skip class. You need to nail down a routine. A bathroom pass, a sign-out sheet, or a routine that you or your school designates needs to be explained in the first few minutes of day one.

Wrangling, Not Strangling

After you get their attention, another crucial task is to introduce guidelines for behavior that you all follow. Commonly referred to as rules, norms, guidelines, a classroom constitution—call it what you like—there should be a system in the classroom so that everyone, including yourself, knows what is and is not acceptable.

I have never started a school year with a preprinted list of rules. One of the first tasks of the first day of school is to ask your students, "What should the rules be for our class? What laws should we create?" Every year I am surprised by the innovative answers and also by the students' interest in building a classroom environment similar to what I had envisioned. Students want an environment that promotes physical and emotional safety, allows for innovation and risk taking, and feels and is respectful. When we form rules together, everyone buys into the design of life in the classroom. But this doesn't mean that the rules don't need to be enforced. Everyone, including myself, needs to be reminded. Recently, I was kicked out of my own classroom for eating because I was breaking an agreed-upon rule. I had to eat in the hallway while my class laughed and went on working without me.

Creating classroom guidelines together builds harmony and community. The first day of class without fundamental class rules is like a street with pedestrian, bike, and automobile traffic and no laws about where to walk, ride, or drive—and no traffic lights. Establishing operational structure immediately goes a long way to encouraging participation, comfort, and understanding. In fact, ensure that you and your students know the school rules (which often include no running in hallways and no eating in classrooms) as you begin to develop classroom guidelines. Keep in mind that guidelines that result from consensual agreements are not threatening. Instead, they are supportive and help everyone live peacefully in the classroom. Many teachers assume the guidelines and consequences are for their sanity, but that is less than half of the pie. The groundwork helps students understand how you would like them to treat each other. During the first week, illuminate this fact: "These rules are not just for you and me but for all of us."

"Why do we have laws?" Andrea asks. Her students' answers, although they vary depending on age, are consistent with the fact that they believe laws and rules help to keep people respectful, safe, and equal. "And that is exactly why we have rules in the classroom," she told them. "For that exact reason, and not just for how you treat me and how I speak to you, but how we all treat each other." Andrea told me, "We spend time role modeling the rules we created so the kids are very clear that this is about all of us, the entire community, including me."

With the development of class guidelines comes the need to develop consequences. Your students know what is fair and you can add or subtract consequences as you develop the rules. But never forget that consequences are necessary.

"No matter how well-behaved the class is, I always enforce an agreed-upon consequence the first week of school. It is a gentle reminder to the entire class that I want to promote a consistent, fair, and equal system in my classroom." When my colleague Liz told me this, I thought she was being unreasonably

strict. "It's unfair to my students not to understand that there are consequences in the classroom, just like there are in life. Letting them know the first week of school just adds an extra layer of understanding, and where they stand with me and me with them. And with some classes that are wilder, it happens faster; with others, it might take three days. But it always happens." If you saw her classroom later in the year, a lab of fun learning, you would see it makes sense and was a clear way to promote responsibility quickly.

Creating class guidelines as a group, instead of presenting a list of rules that students must follow, helps to establish a positive mood in the classroom. If you are willing to spend the time and energy to develop guidelines as a class, the guidelines will help to produce a sense of community and equality that will extend far beyond the first hours of the school year. The work you put in will pay off in dividends later.

Establishing Routines

Without basic routines, basic needs can cause havoc and chaos. Consider how you want students to enter the classroom every day. Do you want them to line up outside the door or come right in and sit down? Decide before the first day and then make the routine clear, perhaps by practicing it.

The same goes for how you want students to exit your classroom. Do you want students to line up? If they do, in one line or two? Where? Inside the classroom or outside? You can figure out ways to have students line up silently. Perhaps you'll choose by height, which can be used when attending town hall meetings so the taller kids are not sitting in the front of the shorter kids, or maybe by birthday. Other ideas are by first letter of their last names, mode of transportation used to get to school, where they live, or anything positive that applies to the lives of your students.

Find out what school leaders and colleagues expect and also what works for you, your students, and your classroom's location. By the way, if the teacher next door has been asking her students to line up outside her door for 45 years and there isn't room for yours, you'll have to ask your students to gather in your classroom or figure something else out. Fast!

Taking a Load Off

Kids' backpacks are heavy, and may be especially so on the first day of school. Truthfully, kids carry a lot in their pockets, purses, and backpacks, whether they are in 1st grade or 8th grade. Because you've designed the classroom to meet storage needs, you can tell your students where they can store their personal belongings and materials. Then, as you slowly introduce materials and manipulatives into the classroom routine, your students will learn where to store those things and how the classroom is organized.

One year I assumed my 4th and 5th grade students would know where to put pencils away, namely in the bins on the tables. But I hadn't introduced them to the bins. When I said, "Put the pencils away," no one knew where that was or what I meant. Some students put them in backpacks, assuming the pencils were gifts. Others put them in the table bins, and still others got up and gave me the pencils, thereby causing a massive traffic jam. A few students left the pencils on the table and they eventually rolled onto the floor.

Now that your room is filled with students and materials, what is the first activity you are going to have them do? Whether your students will work independently or in small groups, start by introducing the materials they will need and how to access them, use them, and put them away. On this first day or in this first week, do not make the activities dependent upon what your students bring in to do an activity. Make sure that the materials are available and ready to go.

Checklist

- ☐ Signaling for attention
- ☐ Wrangling, not strangling
- ☐ Establishing routines
- ☐ Taking a load off

Now that these are established, you and your students will be ready to do an activity. That's in the next section.

Start Slowly and Smoothly

You've figured out how to get your students' attention and they know how to get yours. Classroom guidelines and consequences are in place. Everyone seems to understand the basic routines of the classroom, at least for now (some will be forgotten at least once a week). Now, what do you do?

Jumping into your first math lesson will bore your students. They need some time to practice working and integrating the guidelines they helped to create before diving into the curriculum. Instead, do something that lets them get to know each other and you to get to know them. Do some fun activities to get students moving and to help you set some clear boundaries as a teacher. In this chapter we will cover:

- Getting students involved
- Establishing boundaries and extending a hand
- Understanding expectations

Getting Students Involved

With the excitement of the first week of school, your students are going to be filled with energy. Letting them sit for too long is asking for problems, so plan a few activities to get them thinking and working sooner rather than later. As I've mentioned, you should involve your students in developing rules and consequences, but there are other activities that can encourage your students to become engaged.

When I started my second year of teaching, I was determined to put the mistakes I had made in my first year behind me. I had learned what didn't work and was enthusiastic about starting the year strong. Consequently, I tried to squeeze way too much information into the first few mornings of school. With his head lowered, one of my 1st grade students raised his hand and asked, "Are you going to talk this much every day or can we have some fun and do something?" After that we got right to doing activities. Lesson learned. I had to wait until the third year to start off right.

If you teach young students, let them create or decorate a nametag. In the process, you'll be able to teach them where to find and store the markers and colored pencils and other manipulatives.

When I made the jump from teaching 5th grade to teaching 6th to 8th graders, I had to change. I planned to start the year using many of the activities I had employed when teaching elementary school. Although the activities worked with the 6th graders, the 7th and 8th graders would have nothing to do with them. They stared at me like I was from another planet when I suggested making nametags. Quickly adjusting to their level of maturity, I asked them to create graffiti-style cards featuring their initials. It worked!

Older students can rearrange books in the class library. Ask students to take a stack of books to their desks and arrange them alphabetically or by author. For nonfiction, they can separate titles by subject and in the meantime get to know the books that are in classroom.

Decorating tip. Many teachers, anxious to get their rooms completely decorated before school starts, purchase premade charts. I like to create charts out of the information that my students and I discuss, such as birthdays, favorite colors, preferred musicians or genres, and books read over the summer. If you are teaching a single subject, ask your students to produce KWL (What I Know, What I Want to Know, What I Learned) charts in small groups to get them to interact. If you plan several activities that include charts or visual components, you'll see that having students create posters builds community, introduces routines through action, and decorates your classroom in the first week of school.

Another good activity is having students write a note to their parents or families about what they did on the first day of school. Even the youngest students can draw a picture to accomplish the same goal. And this activity helps to build a bridge between school and home.

All these activities, whether used with kindergarteners or 7th graders, need to be modified and differentiated for the specific age and population. Most important, sprinkle these activities throughout to ensure no one's foot falls asleep from sitting too long. Watching your students work on and complete these activities can serve as informal assessments, as well.

Establishing Boundaries and Extending a Hand

During the first week of school, you will be giving a lot of energy and effort to your students. As you extend yourself, it is important to establish routines for your students and yourself. You'll need to set boundaries that help everyone understand what you are and are not willing (or able) to do.

During my first year teaching middle school, I allowed a few kids to eat lunch in my classroom early in the term. It was one day so it was fine. Well, little did I know that the word spread that I was "cool" with allowing kids in my classroom at lunch. The first day it was five kids. The next it was 10. And the following day 30 kids were asking to eat in my room. It ended there. If I had been clear about how many kids could come to eat, or offered a sign-up sheet, the outcome would have been different. Instead, I ended up disappointing a bunch of kids by denying them entrance.

The school year is not a sprint. It is a long, slow walk. Take it that way or you'll be out of breath and exhausted by the end of the month. It is easier to add freedoms than to take them away, so be clear with your boundaries at the beginning of the year. Before answering the following questions, find out the school policies so that you save yourself time and effort. Here are a few questions to ask yourself about lunch and recess time:

- Do you want students to come into your classroom for lunch?
- Do you only allow access to your room for specific reasons?
- Is lunch or recess in your room a privilege? A punishment? Or can it be both?

- Do you plan to eat in the cafeteria with your students? Regularly?
- Are you available after school? How often? One day per week? Every day? Is there a sign-up sheet?
- Can students do homework during lunch or recess or do some students have to do it then? Where can they work?

It is fun to surprise your students and eat in the cafeteria with them, but be careful of setting up false expectations. You'll also need to learn what is expected and what is forbidden. In some situations, teachers are required to walk students to lunch, in other schools the students are allowed to find their own way. Not knowing the rules can cause hurt feelings and exhaust you.

Understanding Expectations

It's important to remember that you are not a superhero. Find out what your supervisor and colleagues expect of you before school starts, including what you need to do about signing in at school and what the office staff expects of you. Understanding standard procedures and expectations will help you keep your energy levels high and your day unburdened by unnecessary tasks. For example, you may be expected or required to work with students after school or participate in school community events, such as fundraisers, after-school celebrations, or committees. If you start out by following the guidelines and remain consistent, community members, students, faculty, and staff will be clear about what they can expect from you. Acting on your responsibilities is important as a member of the school community. Your compliance and actions will communicate to your colleagues and administration that you are dependable and willing to play your role—and will help you determine what extra tasks you are willing or able to do. Remember, each school is entirely different regarding schedules, systems, and expectations.

Taking the initiative to do more than is required within your school community is the work of an inspired educator. Just be sure you can keep it up and don't overburden yourself. Giving extra effort to your administration is key as well—but only if it doesn't take away from your work as a classroom teacher.

Checklist

- ☐ Getting students involved
- ☐ Establishing boundaries and extending a hand
- ☐ Understanding expectations

I didn't forget about setting up clear expectations and boundaries with parents. They are an extension of the work you do in the classroom and that is another key aspect of the first week of school. That's up next.

Connect with Families

Although parents and significant caregivers are usually invisible to you during the school day, it's imperative to establish a connection with them during the first week of school and to nurture the relationship throughout the year. At the very least, it's a good to explain what parents, families, and caregivers can expect their child's daily life at school to be like and to encourage their participation. To best connect with these significant people, I suggest the following:

- Assigning students to write a letter
- Writing a teacher's letter
- Asking for a parent or family letter

Schools can be daunting to some parents. You have the power to reduce the intimidation factor and to have that effort pay off when you need classroom volunteers, field-trip chaperones, or fundraising support. You won't get every family to participate, but you can lay the groundwork so that all families feel that they can contribute and that their efforts are valued. Make a point to reach out to parents and families during the first week of school so that they understand you are making an effort to include them in their child's education—and that you're not just fulfilling your requirements of back-to-school night.

Assigning Students to Write a Letter

By the end of the first day of school, I'm exhausted from the excitement of meeting new students, the energy of the students as they come together, and the buzz as we figure each other out. Although I know I will be too tired to write a quick note to send home, I think it's valuable for families to have something to discuss that's directly related to the important first day of the school year. To facilitate this idea, whether teaching one class (elementary) or a few (middle), I ask my students to write a quick note to their families. Who better to write about what happened on the first day of school? The note can be about what happened in class on the first day, what we are going to study, a new person they met, the classroom, or me. They must return this note the next day with a signature from home, which helps form a school-to-home connection the first week. A clear line of communication will make you, your students, and their families more comfortable.

Keep in mind that a student's family is a source of information for understanding his personality and habits. Family structures can be different for each student. Therefore it's crucial to be aware of and sensitive to family structures. The person who signed the letter, whether a parent, older brother or sister, aunt, grandmother, cousin, or family friend, is likely in charge at home. Be sure to stay flexible. And if the note isn't returned, find out why. Maybe it was left in a backpack or on the kitchen table—or maybe no one else was home. Finding out why the note wasn't returned can help you glean important information about your student.

Writing a Teacher's Letter

A letter from you can help parents to better understand general classroom policies, what to expect for their child and, most significantly, introduce you. Your introduction can be a short paragraph, but do share information about your teaching experience or professional training and a few things about your personal history, such as where you are from and how long you have lived there. Details about hobbies or things you like to do offer a window into your out-of-school interests and will make it easier for parents to identify with you as a person and talk with you when they need to contact you or voice concerns.

For years I packed the letter home with a lot of information, including my personal introduction, classroom policies, school information, the school's emergency card, and a million requests. I needed some forms back for the school and some forms for me, including a request for personal information about their child and potential volunteer opportunities. I received about half the needed information back the next day and then the rest would come in over the next two to three weeks in dribs and drabs. Then I had an epiphany: this was a lot of paperwork I was asking for! I was overwhelming some families. So I tried something new: I split up the packet into three smaller ones, each with some form or information I needed or wanted from them. I sent these out over the first week or two and the forms came back faster.

Your letter to home should include important dates (e.g., back-to-school night, parent-teacher conferences), the schedule for the school day with arrival and dismissal times, your classroom schedule, homework policies (e.g., due dates and make up allowances), classroom policies (e.g., whether water bottles are allowed; classroom visitation guidelines), and volunteer opportunities.

The method of communication and verification. Your letter should include information about the form of two-way communication that you plan to use with families, whether a homework folder, an e-mail address, or the school phone number. Do not give out your personal phone number or e-mail address. Use a work specific e-mail address to keep your personal and professional lives separate, especially so that you are not reading or sending parent messages while you're out on Friday night. You need to deliver contact information to your students' families as soon as possible—and make it available to your students as well. Keep in mind that you want to test the method of communication before you need it.

"I test out the method of communication the first week or so of school, whether I have gotten it from the parents or from the prior year's academic file, before I have to use it for something really important," says Ted, a 1st grade teacher with experience teaching 1st through 6th grades during his 20-year career in public schools. "I want to know that the communication portal, whatever it may be—note home, e-mail message, or phone—works. It takes some extra time that first week or so but it is really worth it, especially for families who do not have access to the Internet in their home or use a relative's phone. These are the families who are used to being excluded from school information. Receiving a phone call from their child's teacher or even a message of greeting can mean a lot. And I always keep the phone conversation entirely positive. Always."

After you have received contact information for each family, ask for them for some information to help connect them with the classroom. See the next section for ideas.

Asking for a Parent or Family Letter

Whether you send an e-mail message or a photocopied letter, ask parents or caregivers to respond with a quick note to you about their child as a student. Invite them to reply by sharing whatever they would like about their child or asking them to respond to an outline that you provide. Here are some topics that you may want to offer:

- Strengths and achievements
- Highlights from the previous school year
- Areas for improvement

The school experiences of the families are inevitably varied. If you include an opportunity for the parents and significant adults to share their own school experiences, specifically about the grade you are teaching, these memories can shed light upon their reluctance or willingness to participate in their child's school life. They might write about a teacher they loved or hated. You can always mention that information in a passing conversation to make them feel more comfortable. For example, "Don't worry. I read what you wrote. Don't expect three hours of homework like Ms. Doe gave you when you were in 6th grade. That sounds awful!" Your acknowledgment of what they shared introduces an immediate feeling of empathy, which can help parents and families feel included in the classroom community and increase their comfort level with you. Remember, teachers can be intimidating. Believe it or not, in a lot of families you're a superhero!

Although English may not be spoken in a student's home, technology and other resources allow teachers to overcome this obstacle when communicating with a student's family. Parents can be an incredible resource and obtaining their participation is one of many keys to your success as a teacher. Making communication with families a priority sends a message to families that you want them to be part of their child's education.

Checklist

- ☐ Assigning students to write a letter
- ☐ Writing a teacher's letter
- ☐ Asking for a parent or family letter

Let's wrap it up with a few more ideas and then you're off to plan your first week.

Epilogue

It's Friday at 3:30. You just finished the first week of school. The weekend has officially begun but you remain in your classroom preparing for next week, reflecting on those first moments with your new class. In addition to other achievements, you have accomplished these milestones:

- Arranged your physical classroom
- Established a tone that will be characteristic of your teaching
- Created and practiced routines, systems, and class guidelines
- Facilitated activities to get students thinking, talking to each other, and creating a community
- Reached out to parents and families and offered multiple avenues for school-and-home communications

It was a busy week. The first week of school is critical and lots of fun, but the end of the week gives you the opportunity to reflect: What went well? What didn't go as you wanted it to? What would you like to change?

I have never experienced a first week of school that was "perfect." I don't know what perfect is. There are always routines I want to tweak, like changes to the classroom setup and seat assignments or lack thereof. There are activities I want to alter for the following year and ones I'd like to do during the second week. There are families I didn't get in touch with. There is always more. The first Friday is an incredibly valuable time to contemplate and grow.

Right now, week number two is only two and a half days away. You know so much more than you did and now you want to improve, change, and be ready. You want to establish an energy in the class and prove your commitment to the students. The end of the first week is a real chance to consider the changes you would like to make before the concrete sets and it becomes harder to make adjustments to your classroom routines.

Change. But how do you make changes when routines have already been established? It's easy. You clearly state that is exactly what you and the students are about to do: "Last week was great. Now I want to do something new that will be even better." Or if it was obvious that you fell on your face when establishing a routine, then say that, too: "That system didn't work that well, so this week we'll change and do this." Let the students in on what did and didn't work. Tell them what they did well and what they need to improve upon, just like you're doing for yourself. Never be afraid to change what didn't work.

Change and improvements can apply to anything, including a routine that you explained to parents or a system you set up for yourself. Don't keep doing something that doesn't work or doesn't fit the kind of teacher you are or want to be. For example, if other teachers tell you to hold your morning meeting first thing but at least five of your students generally arrive later, then plan the meeting for 9:30 a.m. when everyone has arrived. Do what works for you, your students, the class community you are constructing, and the culture of the school. Doing something because you think it is the right way when it obviously doesn't work is a recipe for disaster, and indeed will be far harder to change as the year goes on.

During my first year teaching digital arts in middle school, I had students doing some of their work in notebooks. They carried the notebooks, along with laptops, around the room. They jotted notes in their notebooks and then transferred everything to their laptops. After the first week of school, I could see it wasn't working. Kids were confused about where they should write things down, and at the same time I was bragging that we would have a "paperless classroom." But I didn't give up. I tried to make the notebooks a part of the classroom, even though they obviously were not a good fit. Finally, in December, one of my students said, "This is supposed to be a paperless, digital class, and we are still carrying notebooks everywhere. Let's commit and make it work." I should have given it up the first week. As the weeks went on it was harder and harder for me to let go. So much work was stored on paper. Following my student's lead, however, I devoted a week to becoming paperless and that made life easier for everyone. I wish I had done that the minute I saw the problem. Waiting to make an adjustment is a mistake I will not make again.

Celebrate and capitalize on victories. It's equally as important to congratulate yourself for what did work. Don't let the first week turn into the ninth before celebrating your victories. Teaching is not easy. While incredibly gratifying, the demands can be relentless and flat out hard to meet. You need to learn to be your own friend—a friend who celebrates large and small successes and reflects on what can be improved.

Make a list of what went well the first week of school. Note routines and activities that went well. Review the positive contact you experienced with parents and remember the inspiring conversations among students that you were privy to. Write these in your calendar or planner to review when you are having a tough moment later in the year.

When I taught elementary school, at the end of every day I asked students, "What did you learn today?" The list was both predictable and totally surprising. Not confined to the academic, the list would turn into a lesson about what we were learning. I also did this activity with myself, reflecting upon what I had learned. I try to find a moment to reflect and make my practice better throughout the entire year but I especially make a commitment to do that the first week.

Use your wins during the first week of school to inspire you for the second week. Build on them. If lining up in the hallway went especially well, repeat it and then challenge your class to do it independently. Find ways to celebrate these victories and use them as the building blocks of your classroom community.

Motivation. The first week of school is one of the most exciting of the entire year and you want to put a lot of energy into the planning and execution. Let your motivation as a teacher shine through in everything you do and your students will be more excited than you are to be starting school. Remind yourself:

- Passion is transmittable
- Enthusiasm and commitment are contagious
- Self-reflection and self-congratulation are the tools of those who excel

If you start the week with these reminders, you'll be off to an excellent school year. Good luck—and have fun!

To give your feedback on this publication and be entered into a drawing for a free ASCD Arias e-book, please visit **www.ascd.org/ariasfeedback**

ASCD | arias™

ENCORE

STARTING SCHOOL RIGHT

One of the biggest challenges of the first week of school is keeping track of what you covered and what you didn't, whether you ran out of time or forgot. It is an action-packed week that can go by so quickly that you may realize you only covered half of what you intended to do. That probably means one of two things: you were on a roll and having too much fun to notice what was missed or you were too stressed to take stock of anything.

It's important to prioritize the primary objectives. After establishing an understanding of the school's and classroom's guidelines and rules with your students, you'll need to decide which routines and activities take priority. What is important but not crucial? Here are my suggestions of how to separate these objectives and how to act on them.

Class Routines

Sometime during the first week of school you must get these routines into place:

- Calling and responding (how you get students' attention)
- Raising hands or fingers (how students get your attention)
- Asking for bathroom privileges and appropriate procedures (use a pass or note or other system)
- Storing and accessing coats and backpacks

- Accessing needed materials
- Entering the classroom
- Exiting the classroom

These routines are needed immediately and are strictly functional, meaning they help the whole class operate in an efficient, safe manner. Introduce other routines and systems as you need them, including homework, manipulatives, and more involved systems.

Rituals

I like to establish rituals that will continue throughout the year. These are practices that, as they become familiar, the students will expect every day. These rituals not only create consistency, but they help to define your classroom culture. I often use these rituals:

- Reviewing the daily or class schedule
- Gathering for a morning or daily meeting
- Assigning a "do now" activity for students to complete each day as they enter the classroom
- Singing a song to begin the day (for younger grades)
- Communicating specific breaks (lunch, clean up, dismissal) in the day using a song or nonverbal signal
- Brainstorming at the end of the day about what was learned that day or reviewing information covered that week

These rituals bring closure to particular parts of the day and signal the start of an activity or a transition time.

Families

Reaching out to families the first week of school helps to establish a connection and confidence in the relationship between home and school during the year to come. It is crucial to remember that although you may be anxious about connecting with families, many times your students' parents or guardians are more nervous than you can imagine. As a teacher, you play a powerful role in their child's life and are in charge of the well-being and education of their child. You can begin to forge a connection the first week of school by doing these things:

- Sending a letter home that provides information about you, the class, and what parents can expect (see the section on Writing a Teacher's Letter). A simple letter the first week of school can help build a bridge that can play a very powerful role in the lives of your students. The letter is not intended to be comprehensive, but it is meant to begin to form the relationship.
- Requesting that parents or families send you a note with their perspective about their child's academic tendencies and history.
- Asking parents or caregivers to tell you about their experience as a student—a parent's experience as a student can cast much light on his or her attitude toward school.
- Asking students to write a letter to their parents or caregivers about what they learned and what they expect to learn this first week, which is to be read and

signed by their parent, guardian, or person in charge at home.

- Writing an e-mail message or note or making a phone call to your students' parents. Parents are usually grateful to know if there is an easy way to communicate with their kid's teacher.
- Asking for a few family photos from each student in the class. This activity can involve parents who are likely to send in a copy of a family photo that they like. Although photo requests are often done in lower grades, it is useful as a family involvement strategy at any level.

These ideas are, of course, not all-inclusive of what you must address during the first week of school. Use them to inspire you to think about this intensely exciting and demanding time and what will work for you, your school, and the community. Use these ideas as a springboard to form a first week of school that is a winner for everyone involved. Doing so will set a positive direction for the months to come.

Related Resources

At the time of publication, the following ASCD resources were available (ASCD stock numbers appear in parentheses). For up-to-date information about ASCD resources, go to www.ascd.org. You can search the complete archives of *Educational Leadership* at http://www.ascd.org/el.

ASCD EDge®
Exchange ideas and connect with other educators interested in various education topics, along with New & Student Teachers, on the social networking site ASCD EDge at http://ascdedge.ascd.org.

Print Products
A Better Beginning: Supporting and Mentoring New Teachers edited by Marge Scherer (#199236)

How to Help Beginning Teachers Succeed, 2nd ed., by Stephen P. Gordon and Susan Maxey (#100217)

Peer Coaching to Enrich Professional Practice, School Culture, and Student Learning by Pam Robbins (#115014)

Qualities of Effective Teachers, 2nd ed., by James H. Stronge (#105156)

ASCD PD Online® Courses
An Introduction to the Whole Child (#PD13OC009M)

Classroom Management: Building Effective Relationships, 2nd ed. (#PD11OC104M)

For more information: send e-mail to member@ascd.org; call 1-800-933-2723 or 703-578-9600, press 2; send a fax to 703-575-5400; or write to Information Services, ASCD, 1703 N. Beauregard St., Alexandria, VA 22311-1714 USA.

About the Author

Otis Kriegel, an elementary and middle school teacher for more than 15 years, has taught in dual language (Spanish/English and German/English), monolingual, and integrated coteaching classrooms. He has taught in public schools in New York City, Los Angeles, San Francisco, and Berlin, Germany. He has an M.S. Ed. in Bilingual Education from the Bank Street College of Education, was adjunct faculty at the Steinhardt School at New York University, and a guest lecturer at the Bank Street College. Kriegel's first book, *Everything a New Elementary School Teacher REALLY Needs to Know (But Didn't Learn in College)* (Free Spirit Publishing, 2013) was inspired by the program he created, How to Survive Your First Years Teaching & Have a Life, which he has given to preservice, new, and veteran teachers as well as principals, administrators, and coaches. He continues to lecture at universities, teacher education programs, K–8 schools, and major educational conferences. To contact Kriegel or for more information about speeches, programs, workshops, and other publications, visit www.otiskriegel.com.

THE WHOLE CHILD

ASCD's Whole Child approach is an effort to transition from a focus on narrowly defined academic achievement to one that promotes the long-term development and success of all children. Through this approach, ASCD supports educators, families, community members, and policymakers as they move from a vision about educating the whole child to sustainable, collaborative actions.

Starting School Right: How do I plan for a successful first week in my classroom relates to the **safe, engaged,** and **supported** tenets.

WHOLE CHILD
TENETS

1 HEALTHY
Each student enters school healthy and learns about and practices a healthy lifestyle.

2 SAFE
Each student learns in an environment that is physically and emotionally safe for students and adults.

3 ENGAGED
Each student is actively engaged in learning and is connected to the school and broader community.

4 SUPPORTED
Each student has access to personalized learning and is supported by qualified, caring adults.

5 CHALLENGED
Each student is challenged academically and prepared for success in college or further study and for employment and participation in a global environment.

LEARN. TEACH. LEAD.